# Street Wise and Alley Raised

### KELLY DOHERTY KIMBERLIN

Street Wise and Alley Raised

Publishing support by SJM Copywriting

Copyright © 2018, Kelly Kimberlin

Published in the United States of America

ISBN-13: 9781790673254

# DEDICATION

I dedicate this book to my family that made me who I am today. To my charismatic father Tom, who showed me how to laugh and cry, to my giving mother Joan, who taught me how to stand strong during the hard times. To my older brothers Mick and Brian, who taught me how to be tough. and to my younger brothers Sean and Terry, who taught me about unconditional love.

# Contents

DEDICATION                                                    i

FOREWORD by Stathy Darcy                                      v

INTRODUCTION                                                  vii

CHAPTER 1 – Southside Girl                                    1

CHAPTER 2 – Archie Bunker For A Dad                           7

CHAPTER 3 – Mini Badass                                       13

CHAPTER 4 – The Glue That Held My Family Together            15

CHAPTER 5 – Teenage Rebel                                    19

CHAPTER 6 – Just A Girl                                       25

CHAPTER 7 – Getting Married                                   29

CHAPTER 8 – People Pleaser                                    35

CHAPTER 9 – Losing My Dad                                     39

CHAPTER 10 – Baby Or No Baby?                                 43

CHAPTER 11 – The Shit Show Continues                         53

CHAPTER 12 – Gary Takes His Turn Falling Apart               57

CHAPTER 13 – Saint Joan Slowly Leaves Us                     63

CHAPTER 14 – What The Hell Happened?                         69

EPILOGUE                                                     73

ACKNOWLEDGEMENTS                                             75

# FOREWORD

*Stathy Darcy*

W omen so often find themselves needing to "do it all" and, far too frequently, find themselves in the midst of chaotic activity for others, doing little, if anything, for themselves. As women, we are told from a young age that others' needs are prioritized, then we sometimes end up married, with children or taking care of our parents – and again, our needs and desires take a backseat. A lot of women don't always find the strength and confidence to redirect the endless energy geared toward ensuring everyone else's happiness.

In this incredibly touching and humorous story of discovering just that strength and confidence, Kelly not only finds herself putting everyone else's needs before hers, she is also constantly transforming her real self to what others need her to be - unquestioning daughter, loyal sister, committed wife, dedicated mother, tireless caretaker. And she almost loses Kelly – who she is, what she wants – in the process. Kelly's journey is one of resilience … a successful trek from disappearing into roles demanded by others to an uncompromising confirmation that her happiness has to be based on her own individualized purpose.

# INTRODUCTION

This book is written from my heart, from deep within my soul. I had to go back to the beginning to see how I became so disconnected from myself. Why was I so sensitive, why was I putting others first before my own happiness? How did I get to be so tough, so angry? Where did all these conditioned thoughts and emotions come from? I had a lot of questions I wanted to answer so I could begin the process of changing my old patterns and to start feeling like myself again. I was tired of beating myself up, I just wanted to love myself unconditionally.

I had no idea that I had a soul that was aching to be heard. I just kept taking life as it was coming to me, one challenge after another. I was so disconnected from my Inner Badass self that I denied myself true happiness, almost to the point of ending my own life.

My father used to tell me that I wasn't as smart as my brothers, but I was street wise and alley raised. I didn't really understand it at the time, but I have come to believe that he knew me better than I knew myself! I had that inner wisdom to be able to handle any challenge I came across, but somehow I got lost along the way.

I believe that we all come into this world fully equipped with what we need to have an expansive life filled with experiences that shape us into the best versions of ourselves. And we do this by staying connected to that inner badass that is connected to the bigger badass, our true source. But when you get disconnected from your authentic self, life tends to be more challenging, more stressful and more chaotic. Sometimes it can lead to illness and despair and you almost feel like you are in some kind of survival mode, just trying to make it through another day. And that is exactly where I ended up after forty-eight years denying my soul the chance to express itself. But when you are truly connected to your soul's purpose, life can bring you more joy and true inner peace, even through the toughest of times. And that is what I have been working on for the last four years.

There is constantly a nudging from our souls trying to guide us in the right direction, and most of the time we are not paying attention to it. We get into a habit of doing what we think others in society see as the right thing for us. But instead, all we have to do is sit quietly and ask ourselves the questions we need answers for, and then pay attention and be aware of the guidance we are getting from within.

The problem is we are so busy distracting ourselves from our inner GPS because we don't want to know just how unhappy and unfulfilled we really are. I think it's too scary for people to look deep within themselves and ask themselves what they would love to create in their lives. Some of us don't think we are worthy of greater things, that we aren't smart enough, that we don't have the capability to do more, that there isn't enough to go around. We tend to settle and live mediocre lives because we are afraid to get out of our comfort zones.

When we get excited about something bigger and better in our life, some of us tend to kick it to the side because we are afraid that it will never happen. We don't believe that it is possible, that we are capable of creating anything different, so we stay in our comfort zone. Even if your comfort zone is difficult, it is what you are familiar with, and the unknown is too scary to even think about. But the alternative is even scarier.

So, in this first book of mine I will be taking you on the journey that I believe took me to rock bottom. I had to go back to see how the decisions and the choices I made, up until then, had created the shit show I was currently living in. I will take you all the way down rabbit hole, exposing everything I went through, and in the next book, "How my Inner Badass saved my life", you will see that when I owned all my decisions and started making choices that served me things started to turn around.

*Street Wise and Alley Raised*

# CHAPTER 1

*Southside Girl*

My Dad used to tell me, "You're not as smart as your brothers, but you are street wise and alley raised. You'll be just fine." I really didn't know what he was talking about at the time, but as I grew older I came to understand that I had a lot of common sense and would be able to handle just about anything. Well, that was true up until 2014, when I turned 48.

Let me start at the beginning. I grew up in South St. Louis City where I really wasn't allowed to go off my block on most days. That didn't make much sense when my parents allowed me to take the public bus to school a couple miles away. I guess they thought our neighborhood was a little rough and I have to agree with them. The thing that I hated the most was when I was chased by loose dogs on the street. One mutt actually busted through a screen door just to chase me down and try to bite my ass, so I actually jumped on the top of a car to avoid him. Talk about a threat.

I was the middle child, the only girl with four brothers to deal with. My oldest brother Mick was seven years older than me and he left me pretty much alone. Brian, three and a half years older, loved to tease the hell out of me. There was one night, during dish duty, that I found myself in the trash can. I called out to my Mom,

*My Dad, Mom, Brian, myself, Mick, Sean, and Terry*

1

"Brian put me in the trash can!" Since Brian was her favorite, she simply told me, "If you would stop irritating your brother, maybe you wouldn't be in the trash can."

*Brian's grin could win Mom over every time.*

And there he stood with that shit-eating grin on his face. God forbid that he acted like he really liked me (because that would be weird, right?), older brothers are born to aggravate their younger sisters. That's how our entire family operated; we lived to tease and make fun of each other. That was our entertainment. You had to be tough skinned, and if you were going to cry, it had better be in your room later when you were alone.

I also had a brother seven years younger named Sean. He was chunky and so damn cute. He was even known for walking on his toes. Then there was Terry, nine years younger than me, just as adorable with this blond curly hair and big blue eyes. He was so smart, he could recite the Magic Fish story, a book we used to read him, word for word at the age of four. I couldn't resist being with the younger boys all the time, because they were nice to me. So the older ones were known as the "Big Guys" and Sean and Terry were the "Little Guys", and then there was me, all alone in the middle.

At least that's how I felt most of the time. Sure, I spent a lot of time playing with the Little Guys, but I spent the rest of my time pretty much in my own 5'x8' room. I did have one friend in the neighborhood, named Tammy, and we spent some time together, so that was good. And it was a lot safer than playing with my older brothers. Because they always came up with crazy ideas they would call "games", like tackle sledding. We would take turns launching down the hill at Bellerive park, off Broadway, and when it was your turn to go down, everyone else playing would try and tackle you off the sled. If you survived that, your sled was headed straight down Broadway and you had to be able to dodge any cars coming at you.

We also played King of the Hill at Carondelet park every Tuesday night when our Dad played horseshoes. Someone would get on the top of the slide, to be "King of the Hill" and the other players would try and tackle him from the top. There must be something about boys and tackling, they loved it. They also played a lot of hockey back in the day and I caught several of those pucks with the side of my head.

Dungeon Tag was another favorite neighborhood game that was actually a lot of fun. We would have teams and one team was "it" and had to find and tag the other team and put them in the dungeon, no tackling involved. And we had this huge Veterans of Foreign Wars hall next to us with a great entrance for a dungeon. It was a fairly safe game to play until the day I was running and tripped on the marble sidewalk in the back. I cut my knee open pretty good. Actually, *really good*. It was so bad my brothers had to go get Dad, who was in the middle of a card game and also in the middle of a pretty good buzz. So Dad and his buddies come out and they decide I had to go get stitches, and then they had to decide which one was the most sober and could drive me to the hospital.

Growing up like this, you get tough, you don't take too much bullshit. It's a slow process where you begin to think, *Hmmm, I might have to take care of myself. I'm probably going to have to become a hard ass*, and I proved it time and time again. I mean, you couldn't be a puss walking around in South St. Louis, you had to at least act like you weren't scared.

Especially the time when I was in second grade, walking home from school after picture day. My mom attempted to do my hair and it was a little puffy.

The fifth grader walking home with us kept calling me Herman Munster, from *The Munsters*, and I told him to stop it. I told him several times. I thought I was being pretty generous, but he continued to make fun of me. Finally I took my lunchbox and swung it across his face, and there was blood everywhere. I split his face open pretty good, from his nose down to his lip. I think this is what my Dad meant when he called me "street wise and alley raised".

*Second grade – puffy hair, didn't care.*

I had to be tough, there was no other way to survive being the only girl. Crying never worked. I had such stomach pains one Halloween and started to cry, and my Dad thought giving me a shot of Irish whiskey would toughen me up and solve the problem. Well it didn't. Instead, the whiskey gave me convulsions and I missed trick-or-treating.

They waited until the next day to take me to the doctor, even after the convulsions, and when the doctor saw me, he immediately sent me to the hospital to have emergency surgery because my appendix was getting ready to burst. A burst appendix can kill a person, so it was serious. After surgery I was at Cardinal Glennon for a week so they could keep an eye on me. *My parents left me there!* I would call home and ask if they were coming to see me and my Mom said she had the younger boys at home and couldn't leave them. So I was in the hospital, kind of freaked out, being only 12 years old down there by myself so long! Apparently they thought I was tough enough to handle it. And this is part of my beginning as a MINI BADASS.

One of my favorite memories at 216 Dover was on Christmas Eve. We had the normal fighting going on, like Brian teasing me, Dad getting in Mom's way, but we also had the tradition of stealing our Christmas tree. We would wait until it got dark, put on hats and ski masks, pile into Big Red (that's my Dad's car) and head over to the Venture parking lot where the tree lot was. We would sit there and wait for the attendant to leave and then all jump out of the car, run around the lot looking for a halfway decent tree and throw it on top of Big Red.

In the later years of tree stealing, my brother would be sporting one of those big video cameras on his shoulder to get it on film. Oh how the Doherty's love to watch themselves on film! One night, Big Red didn't start up after we stole the tree and we were stuck in the parking lot. We had to go find a pay phone to call my Mom to come get us in her Cutlass. Piling all of us and the tree into that smaller car was hysterical. I can still hear all the laughter from those times.

*Tree-stealing shenanigans and getting it all on video.*

# CHAPTER 2

*Archie Bunker for a Dad*

M y Dad was an interesting character, to say the least. If you remember the show *All In The Family*, starring Carroll O'Connor as Archie Bunker, this was my father, Tom. He was also known as Duffy down at Anheuser Busch, where he worked as a brewer.

*Tom Doherty*

*Carrol O'Connor as Archie Bunker
(Wikimedia Commons)*

But my Dad had an interesting twist: he liked to drink, and working at the brewery made it easy for him to do it daily. Like all day, 7 days a week. He loved to tell people he worked 7 days a week -- shift work, mind you -- but he never mentioned he had 9 weeks of vacation. And in all those years we only got to go to the Lake of the Ozarks twice for vacation, just two hours away, which was a shit show in itself.

*In the Brewery, tapping right out of the beer tanks.*

On top of all that, he had all these quirks. One of them was nicknames, and most of the time only he knew what they meant. Once he was trying to fix something on the station wagon before we put all the luggage on top of it, and he said to me, "Go get blackie for me."

"What?" I said. *What the hell is a blackie? A paintbrush? A t-shirt?*

"You know, the big wrench downstairs by the tools." Oh, *that* one! Why didn't I think of that? Silly me, I should have known that "blackie" was a wrench, because why wouldn't it be?

But, there was one thing I wished he'd had a better nickname for: all the time he would actually use the word *pee-pee* in conversation! Yep, late at night he would be lecturing the boys on keeping their "pee-pee" in their pants. So glad he never gave *me* the sex talk.

Anyway, on the very last one of those infrequent family trips we took, after all the screaming and yelling just getting the luggage on the top of Big Red, it actually fell off a mile down the highway. Not the pee-pee, *all our luggage*! No kidding, less than a mile, we didn't even make it to the next exit. That may be one of the reasons that was the last trip we took to the Ozarks.

Our regular family vacation included a week of stay-at-home adventures. We went to the Zoo, Grant's farm, or The Spaghetti Factory for dinner (that was exciting because we never went out to dinner), Ted Drewes, and of course a tour of the Brewery. I guess he couldn't stand to be away for a week. Needless to say, this is why I love to travel, because we could never afford to go anywhere and so I have the urge to see everything I missed growing up. He did go on a lot of golf trips with his buddies, which we never minded because it was a little break from the usual chaos at 216 Dover.

Our Archie Bunker had a lot more character. The big thing he had in common was the ridiculous sayings he would come up with. Dad would say, "Did you hear Brian went to the Ozarks and got one of those condoms done there?" We all knew he meant a "condo", but thinking about Brian and condoms made me crack up.

Or he would say, "I would give my right arm to play the piano." I mean, if you don't have a right arm, how are you going to play a piano? Then there was, "Man, that young boy is good looking, he reminds me of myself!" My favorite was, "I think I'm getting that Anheuser's disease." We have pages and pages full of Tomism's. It's so satisfying to go back and read through them and reminisce from time to time.

Most times he had a beer in his hand, a More cigarette in his mouth and his uniform on. Now when I say uniform, I mean, blue jean cut off shorts, no underwear, and a white tank top, or no shirt at all. This is what he would throw on after getting out of the Brewery cellars and come home to a house with no air conditioning. It was hot, and that was all he could handle. I mean, we had shirtless fishing, shirtless digging, shirtless birthday parties, shirtless deck building, you name it, he did it shirtless.

What I couldn't handle was him lying on the couch sideways (with no underwear, remember) and his boys would be hanging out. I can't tell you how many times my Mom had to tuck them back in after hearing me scream, "Mom! Dad's balls are hanging out. Do something!" And Joanie, as my Dad like to call her, would come in and tuck those puppies right back into his short shorts.(No, I do not have a picture. Consider that my gift to you!)

Our Dad did threaten us a lot about getting in trouble at school. We knew if we got in trouble then we were going to get it double when we got home. I know my father and his brothers were always in trouble, so I guess he wanted better for us. I was pretty good in grade school, didn't have too many issues, until I got caught smoking a cigarette on the playground. OH BOY! I was a little nervous to go home after they had called my parents to inform them of my misbehavior because I really had never gotten in trouble before.

I guess I lucked out that day, because they were having one of those infamous after-funeral parties at our house. I think one of my aunts had died, I can't remember. But I do remember that I think my Dad just shook his head and said, "What the hell were you thinking?" And then went right back to his "grieving". So I thought to myself, maybe they were idle threats, and maybe I don't have to be a goody two-shoes at school. The pressure was off.

My Dad was doing a lot of grieving during my teenage years, I remember we went to lots funerals for my Dad's relatives that had passed. He was one of nine children, and when someone passed we used to spend a couple days at these funeral homes and it was torture for us kids. Not for the adults though. Nope, for them it was a drinking extravaganza, just like the Irish like to do it. They can find a way to celebrate just about anything.

While they were "grieving" we were working. The kids were the ones forced to sneak coolers of alcohol into the funeral parlors. Who is going to stop a kid hauling in a cooler? No one. But I do remember the time that the funeral owner found us drinking at the funeral for my Dad's oldest brother, John Doherty, who was the chief of Detectives for the City of St. Louis for many years. The place was packed. And there was a shit ton of drinking going on, and the funeral director told my Dad that they couldn't drink in the funeral home. My Dad said, "Oh, OK, we will put it in cups."

The director said, "No Mr. Doherty, no drinking at all." Well my Dad proceeded to tell him that we have given them a lot of business and we are going to continue to drink, so go on with yourself. OMG, and people wonder where I get my balls from, it probably shouldn't be that hard to understand. Growing up in a family like this, you tend to follow their lead and toughen yourself up pretty quickly.

Dad also had slight temper and he loved to fight. He grew up fighting. He was kicked out of most of the taverns in South St. Louis because of his attitude. He would even come home occasionally with a black eye, and that kind of thing really freaked me out. It didn't happen that often though; he was a bit of an ass kicker.

I found this out personally one night on our way to get dinner. He had come home pretty lit up and he wanted to go get pizza, so we all hopped in the car. Mom was driving and came to the infamous intersection at the top of our street where a lot of people ran the Stop sign, and on this particular night, a guy ran the sign and almost hit us. That would have been really bad since we never wore seat belts. Well, my Dad jumped out of the car, stomped over to the driver's window, pulled the man out of the window, beat the shit out of him and put his head into the street sewer as we all watched.

Even the neighbors came out to watch the show. I still remember everyone sitting on their porches, like this was an everyday thing. Then my Dad just got back in the car, lit a cigarette and said, "Let's go get pizza." This is the kind of shit that was typical at our house. There were many times we were fighting amongst ourselves too. Dad always liked to threaten that he was going to leave after he had been drinking, and Brian would have to take him down, like literally throw him on the ground. Born fighters I guess. I grew to be pretty defensive myself when someone came at me physically or verbally. I would react pretty fast if I thought I was being attacked. I was becoming like my father and just took this as being normal and "the Doherty way". I didn't know I had a choice to be any different. I thought, *This is what I am born into and this is who I am*.

Oh, and did I mention that my father loved himself? Like *really* loved himself. I mean we couldn't do anything bigger or better than him. He was the king of bringing any story back to him to tell us how wonderful he was. He even thought his feet were beautiful. "Look at my feet Kel, aren't they the prettiest feet you have ever seen?"

Dad passed away years ago, but he's never really gone. I believe our loved ones stick around and check up on us. I am constantly telling Mom and Dad to keep an eye on my kids when they are not with me. And I believe they are!

You see, years after my Dad had passed, I was in Michigan, sitting on a bench at the beach, having an ice cream with my husband Gary and my 2 daughters. A little old lady came up to me and said, "I don't know why I feel the need to tell you this, but you have the prettiest feet." I looked at Gary and said, "Dad is here!" It was just one of many confirmations of that connection we have to those angels watching out for us.

# CHAPTER 3

*Mini Badass*

So back in the day we had to fend for ourselves. There weren't any teachers or parents getting involved, we simply took care of ourselves, that was a given. I remember so many fights at the black top after school. Is that a south side thing? Kids would get in an argument at school and find themselves on a parking lot in our neighborhood, book bags thrown on the ground and a good healthy fight between two kids. This took care of a lot of the bullying.

Sometimes I think that is what we are missing in this soft society. What's wrong with a good clean fight between two people to battle out any issues that we might have? It would put bullies in their place. That's how we did things. I didn't get into many fights, I was a very tall girl and somewhat intimidating for my age. Not too many girls or boys messed with me because I just kept my blood-stained lunch box visible.

This might also be the reason that Mom would send me into the taverns Dad use to frequent, to try and persuade him to come home. Aah, good times. I remember going inside, giving him my sad face, and he would start telling me stories, sometimes just to make me cry. He loved to see me cry. I remember watching movies with him and he would ask, "Kel, is this a one or two handkerchief movie?"

I guess since he cried so easily, he liked to see others cry, and I was an easy target for him. He would start telling me sad stories about why he was drinking and that he was sorry, but he wasn't very interested in leaving with me. Sometimes it worked, sometimes it didn't.

I love when my kids tell me how tough they have it, I just shake my head. *Whatever, kids are so spoiled nowadays.* God forbid they should have to take a public bus back and forth to school. The regular yellow school bus was hard enough on them, and I made them take it up until fifth grade, just so they didn't get too pampered. Unlike me, who had to take the public bus to grade school and high school, and if you missed it, you walked home.

I had to catch the 6:30 am bus, right at the ramp of Hwy 55 and Bates, just up from Broadway. I mean, someone could have easily snatched me up and put me in their car and my family would have never seen me again. I really had to watch my surroundings, so it became natural to be like that. And walking from high school to home three and a half miles, because I missed the bus and didn't want to wait an hour for the next one, wasn't the best thing to do as a young girl. I had several occasions when men got the pleasure of exposing themselves to me on my long walks home. I don't know why I wasn't too scared, all I knew was that I was a pretty fast runner, all blue ribbons in grade school, and I always thought I could out run anyone that tried to mess with me. Except for that damn dog one time that caught up with me and bit me right on the leg! Oh Lordy, the memories.

I just sent my oldest daughter to college last week and she keeps complaining how much she has to walk around campus and I love it! They have been driven around their whole lives and now they actually have to do something. College not only gives a kid an education, independence and a chance to find themselves, but it also gives them a chance to walk their ass off.

Okay, enough of that rant. But I do want to take a minute to explain that this book is not about bashing my amazing parents, this is about how I became a strong little girl with a lot of fight in her, and how I lost her, and then found her again. Don't get your pants in a twist thinking I am complaining, or frustrated, or dislike my parents. They did the best they could with what they had and despite everything we all turned out pretty good! They made me the MINI BADASS that was able to go live her life and become the confident, powerful woman I am today.

# CHAPTER 4

### *The Glue That Held My Family Together*

That would be my mother, Joan. "Saint Joan", that was what my father called her, and I have to agree, she was a saint. Our house could be pretty chaotic at times, but my mom was the one who tried to keep it as normal as possible, and she did it mainly from the kitchen. That's where I remember her being all the time with her little apron on, probably one she made, in that small kitchen cooking up the best meals you have ever tasted. The woman could cook. Even today, Gary still sometimes has the nerve to say, "Can you make it like your mom did?" That would be a no, especially since she made everything with extra butter and cheese. The house

*Joan Doherty*

always smelled like a home cooked meal or a cookie. She was infamous for baking about twenty different varieties of cookies at Christmas time.

She was also the mother that got up in the morning before we left for school, to make three different kinds of peanut butter and jelly sandwiches for our lunches. It was always on white bread, but she used apple butter, grape and strawberry jelly to make sure we were all happy. This was my people-pleasing mother, she loved to do things for everybody all the time. I just happened to pick that damn trait up myself,

15

and it's exhausting, trying to please everyone but yourself. Eventually I had to give that up to save my own life. She always put her family first and I think at the end it took a toll on her.

The sad thing is, I don't remember my mom treating herself too much, maybe having a cold beer in an ice cold mug at the end of her day was a treat to her. Mom's favorite thing to do was dance, so when the church had dances she and Dad always went. I remember her making a dress for every dance because she was so excited. And they would go up to the church basement to party, drink and dance to all hours.

Growing up with an alcoholic father was never easy, and by the way, I don't think he ever admitted he had a problem, and we were never allowed to bring it up. This is just what he saw as normal in his own family and it was typical for him to be drinking all the time. My mother also grew up with a father that drank a lot and he ended up passing away in his forties. As a result of that, my grandmother had to go back to work and my mother was the middle child of three and ended up being the caretaker in her family when she was a teenager. Good Lordy, that's a lot of years to be taking care of everyone around you, but that is who she was and she did a damn good job.

So I can see why my mother wasn't very lovey-dovey. She didn't have time for feelings and problems, she was trying to keep it all together. I didn't really understand that until I got older, I was just a little sad that I didn't feel a lot of love from my mother, especially since I was the only girl. I felt alone a lot and just wanted to talk to someone, have someone tell me that it was all going to be alright, that she loved me and I was the best girl she could have ever had, but that never happened. I now know she didn't have that herself as a child, so she really didn't know how to do it for me.

Time to change the pattern. I consider myself a damn good mother, I love on my kids like they are the most important thing to me, because they are. (Gary, you're next in line, sorry.) I spend as much time as I can with my daughters, we laugh, cry, joke around, curse each other out when we get a chance, and make a lot of memories that hopefully bring joy to them. That is one thing I can say I learned from being sad and lonely, my kids know that I love them unconditionally and I want to be the first one they call, whether they are in trouble (and we have had a lot of that) or they are excited about something. Hopefully my kids will take note and keep the loving pattern going with their own families.

People have so many conditioned patterns from their upbringing that they are unaware of. And if they are aware of them, they don't think they can change the patterns. They just think, *This is how I grew up, so this is the way I am.* My own mom didn't think she could get out of her situation, that was how she saw the world and probably considered it normal. But I am here to tell you that you can change your conditioned behaviors if they no longer serve you. You just have to decide you want something better, and you have to believe you deserve it.

My poor mother was in survival mode most of her life and that makes me sad for her. I appreciate everything she did for our family and I am so glad she kept us together. Mom, I hope you are up in Heaven having everyone else wait on you!! Especially Dad!!

# CHAPTER 5

*Teenage Rebel*

I had been so good all those years in grade school. There was enough going on in the house that I was afraid to cause any more problems. And I also thought if I was really good, maybe my Dad would stop drinking so much or come home more often after work. Eventually, though, I realized it wasn't like I was getting any kind of special recognition for being so good, so, fuck it! I was going to join the fun. That's when I really started to do what I wanted.

I got into high school and met some of my lifelong friends and started doing whatever I pleased, especially when I got to use the car. Now I usually had to share the Plymouth Scamp or the Volkswagen bug with my brothers, so I didn't get to have a car too often, but, there was always Big Red. When Dad wasn't using it, of course. The freedom from driving a car anywhere you want was the most exciting time of my life. I had been pretty sheltered and had kept pretty close to home, so this was the most freedom I have ever had. I took advantage of it.

I never had a curfew, no certain time to come home. That was weird right? I stayed out late most weekends, and I knew when my Dad worked late night shift from 11 pm to 7 am, I could even stay out a little later, because Mom never said anything. I remember one morning, I got home between three and four in the morning and my Dad had gotten home early from work (they had partners that would cover for them). He was sitting in the kitchen, still with his uniform on and a cigarette in his mouth. He said, "What the hell are you doing at three in the morning?"

My smart-ass mouth responded, "Do you really want to know what I was just doing? And what are you doing home anyway?" Yikes! *What was I thinking?*

He just shook his head and said, "Get to your room." Seriously, if it was me, I would have smacked the shit out of myself for talking back like that. Sorry Dad! But I guess I didn't care. He would try and give me trouble about staying out late, drinking, talking back, and I would tell him, "Well I don't have the best example to follow, now do I?" He never had any kind of follow up for that one.

I kept getting a little sassier as I got older. I was just following the example I was seeing. I was even bold enough to just start taking beer right out of the refrigerator down in the basement and drinking it. Now, don't think we had some nice fixed-up basement with drywall, carpet, TV and a refrigerator, and I chugged beers while watching TV in comfort. No, all we had were bare walls, a concrete floor, the washer and dryer, tools and other shit all over the place, and a free standing shower in the middle of it all. Not exactly "Lifestyles of the Rich and Famous".

But that's where I would take a shower because we only had a tub in our one-bathroom home. We all had to go down in that cold dreary basement and shower, naked parts hanging out for anyone in the basement to see. The worst part was getting out, especially in the winter months. It was freezing down there. So to treat myself before I would go out on the weekend, I would grab a beer and drink it while I was in the shower. Then I would grab one or two more and bring them up to my room to pre-party all by myself. I am pretty sure I wasn't the only teenager doing that in the house.

Dad shook his head at me a lot when he didn't approve of certain behavior. He never knew how to handle me, maybe because I was a girl, and he didn't like to pull out the strap on me too much. I do remember that noise though when he pulled it off his pants to whip the boys occasionally. So when I got in trouble he would always say to Mom, "Joan, do something with her." He actually chased me down the street one time because I wouldn't stop cursing, and he couldn't catch me, so he threatened to tear my room up, and I just replied, "*No shit?!*" I was becoming a bit of a wild child.

There was one time when he did more than just shake his head. I came home late one night with two other girls and three guys to go skinny dipping in my own back yard. We must have been pretty buzzed to do that. And I thought since it was late and their bedroom was in the front of the house, they would never know. Boy was I wrong. He must have looked out the back window and did not like what he saw. He came out that back door with a cigarette in his mouth, shotgun in his hand, and of course his cut off shorts. I'll never forget it: he cocked the gun, took his cigarette out of his mouth, and said, "Boys I suggest you get your asses out of that pool right now."

Well, I never saw anyone jump out of a pool that fast. They took off running, and without their clothes on. Then my Dad went *inside*, and locked me *out*. I had to wait for my brothers to come home to let me in. Needless to say, they told me how stupid I was, and to never skinny dip in your own back yard. Lesson learned.

It was pretty quiet the next day. We were really good at not talking about anything that ever happened, we just kind of moved on. So when I wanted to use Big Red again that night, I actually had the balls to ask my Dad for the car. He shook his head, said he was disappointed in me and handed me the keys! Can you imagine that? He was disappointed but there was no punishment. I look back now thinking, did he just not care? Did I just keep doing these things to get his attention, did I want to get punished, so it felt like someone cared? Maybe I just figured if I had to put up with Dad's shenanigans then he had to put up with mine.

I think over the years dealing with my Dad's drinking took a toll on me. I remember staring out my window all the time on the days he didn't come home from work. I would be so worried that something was going to happen to him because I knew he was out drinking somewhere. My stomach would be so upset and I would be praying that he would just come home. Then when he pulled up, the first thing I felt would be relief, but then I would get anxious about what was coming next.

Dad was never one of those that came home and went right to bed. That would have been too easy. For some reason, he loved to preach and cause chaos. Sometimes he would bring buddies home from work and party to all hours of the night. I started resenting him a lot and lost a lot of respect for him. I just didn't care what he thought of me. I loved him like crazy but hated parts of him at the same time. Here's a story I wrote in freshman year about how I felt. This is it, exactly how I wrote it.

Kelly Kimberlin

### Jekyll and Hyde

I am what a person would call a people watcher, I find people extremely interesting. I've come upon two very different individuals, both of whom are parents that live in my neighborhood. Their differences make each of them strong individuals and their similarities make them very unique.

Their names are Joe and Bob, and they enjoy living life to its fullest. Both Joe and Bob love to entertain people and have a good time. They love to barbeque, gamble, play cards and watch old John Wayne Movies. They enjoy their cigarettes and beers as often as they can get them. They both love a game of racquetball and like stopping at the local bar on the way home from work.

The way Bob and Joe differ involves the way they treat others. Joe is very kind, caring and generous. He is the kind of parent who cannot stop giving, he has given all his kids a car, clothes, spending money, and a place to live until they go out on their own. Bob on the other hand is mean and ignorant. He only looks for the faults in people and never has a nice thing to say about anybody. He doesn't care where his kids are or what they are doing. Bob never asks his kids or his wife if they need any help with anything, because he doesn't care. Unlike Joe, who is always there to lend a helping hand, whether its fixing the cars, or helping the boys with their homework.

Joe is the perfect husband and father. He has put his three older children through college and he adores his two little boys like they were gold. He cherishes every minute he spends with his kids. He loves to play baseball, soccer, cards, anything when he finds the time. He also loves the few hours a day he gets to spend with his wife, whether they were riding their bikes, going to yard sales or just going out to eat. Bob only talks to his kids when he wanted to complain about something. He has a tendency to preach at instead of talk with his family. He is constantly telling them what, when and how to do things and to make matters worse he repeats himself. He's always looking for an argument. I think he enjoys yelling and screaming. He's

22

demanding, hateful and jealous of his wife. His children love their mother more and tend to avoid their father as much as possible.

Its amazing, but these two personalities happen to be one person, and that person is my father. He is an alcoholic. I know and love the one who is caring and generous, always there when I need him. I really don't know who the other one is or where he came from. All I know is that Dad brings him home from the bar and I don't like him.

THE END

So this is where I was as a teenager, very confused how one person could be two different people at any given time. There was no warning, but as soon as you looked at Dad you knew which one was coming out. I just wanted to share the way I was feeling back then and the state of mind I was in. I was confused, angry, and really didn't care what happened to me, and that's why I think I got a little wild.

# CHAPTER 6

## *Just A Girl*

So there I was, 17 years old, a senior in high school, and almost a straight-A student, because my Dad insisted on it. Or else I couldn't use the car. And that was important to me, so grades became important. I even went as far as writing down notes on my leg, under my skirt, just to double check my answers, because I wasn't that smart to do it on my own. At least that is what I believed. And I was desperate to use that car to have my fun on the weekends, whatever it took! He only accepted A's and I did get a little bit of a lecture when I got a B, because I was a natural A/B student. It was extremely hard for me to get all A's. Ask my sixth grade teacher. She actually told my mom I wasn't as smart as my brothers, but I "tried real hard." And my mother actually relayed that message to me.

Because of all that I thought something was wrong with me. Now, to be clear, I am not as book-smart as my brothers. Three of them have their Doctorate and the other has a very successful business of his own, but that doesn't make something wrong with me. However, with Dad, Mom, and teachers telling me I wasn't as smart, I eventually started to feel like less. I am smart, just in a different way. I love having all this common sense to figure things out. I understand now that being *street wise and alley raised* suits me perfectly.

In high school, psychology and sociology really lit me up. I absolutely loved those subjects. I thought it would be awesome to be a psychiatrist and I went home to tell my Dad I knew what I wanted to go to college for. I had two older brothers in college, and yes, they got scholarships, but I'm sure my Dad helped them with other expenses. And now it was my turn.

I said, " Dad I want to go to college to be a psychiatrist."

He took his cigarette out of his mouth and asked, "Well who in the hell is paying for that?"

"You can't help me?"

"I am not wasting money on a girl. You'll get married, have kids and waste all your education. Go to the community college and find something there."

That was devastating. I guess I just assumed he was going to help. I was his favorite, his only girl and I thought he thought I was amazing: ballsy, strong, wise, and independent. And so I kind of went into shock and my self-esteem fell off a cliff.

Now my oldest brother Mick was in dental school at the time and he knew that Forest Park Community College had a great Dental Hygiene program. He suggested I get my butt over there and sign up for it since they only take thirty applicants at a time. I had no idea what the hell a dental hygienist was. We only went to the dentist when we had cavities, not for prevention at all.

Anyway, I went and signed up for the Dental Hygiene program, not knowing anything about it. I even remember sitting in class thinking, *What the hell are they talking about?* I had no interest in it, but I finished. Only due to the amazing girls I met. Those ladies have become life time friends that I still see on a regular basis. LOVE YOU GUYS!

I think this was the beginning of following other people's beliefs about what I should be doing with my life and who I was in this world. I was never told that I could be or do whatever I wanted, like we tell our children today. No one talked about following your dreams or finding your soul's purpose! It was about "staying in the box" not rocking the boat, doing what everyone else is doing.

For girls that meant getting a job, find a man, get married, have some kids, buy the big house, get the minivan, and maybe go to Florida once a year. *UGH!* That didn't even sound appealing at the time, I really didn't want to get married at a young age. I had big plans to have my own place, work, travel with friends, date more, really find out who I was and what I really wanted out of life. I was not planning on getting married until I was in my thirties. But somehow I got caught up in this whirl wind of the typical lifestyle and jumped right into the "norm".

By the way, why do so many of us just follow along and try and keep us with the Joneses? Fuck the Joneses. Look what "keeping up" does to people. We are all competing to have the perfect kids, the biggest house, the perfect spouse, make the most money. We're so busy competing with everyone else, we don't enjoy the ride. OK, I am done preaching!

There were so many "have tos" and "should dos" as a young adult that I was losing my ability to decide on what I truly desired. It was like I was disconnected to who I truly was and what I wanted to do in the world.

Hell, I even had trouble picking out clothes to wear when I wasn't in school or at work. I had been in a uniform twelve years in private school. Then I was in a uniform during college for Dental Hygiene clinics and then I always wore what the dental office provided us to wear when I started working. Seriously, it has taken YEARS to find my own style, to really be able to just wear what I want and not what I think other people want me to wear. This kind of "everyone else decides" attitude started showing up everywhere in my life. But now? Now I hate it! And I'll never go back.

So there I was, in the middle of a program that made no sense to me. It did not light me up, and that is a sign of getting disconnected from your Inner Badass and your Inner power, when you no longer follow what you love. I just didn't think I was worthy to follow my dreams anymore.

My father, the one I thought loved me the most, told me I was *just a girl*, and not worthy of his money. I didn't understand: I was his little Rip (another nickname), his only girl, his favorite. I thought he should have been ecstatic that I was excited about something, and the fact that he wasn't at all really impacted me.

I thought that going away to college would have helped me move on from the craziness in my life, that it would have been the time to have some of my own control. I thought, *this is my time*, and when it didn't happen I really was disappointed. But I didn't play the victim, I just went on and completed the dental hygiene program, as uncomfortable as I was. I barely graduated, but I guess that wasn't a big deal. Mom didn't even bother to bring a camera to take pictures, I have no photos of that time. Hell, I don't have a lot of photos of me as a kid anyway. My brothers have all these professional pictures of them and I have ONE.

*Smile? I look like I have to poop.*

This was my one and only professional picture taken as a kid. I don't have room to put all my brother's professional pictures here, that would take up about twenty pages.

Mom told me that I was crying when I got that picture taken, I think I was just one year old, so she never did it again. She also told me I was the ugliest baby she ever had. I was jaundiced, had a half a head of black hair and a broken nose. I guess she didn't want too many pictures of that either.

But the differences I felt between me and my brothers eventually took a toll on my life.

It took me awhile to understand how and why I got disconnected from that little fireball. Eventually, after a couple of decades of being the butt of jokes, my brothers making fun of me, plenty of stories of being ignored by my parents, and now being rejected for college to study psychology and just barely making it through Dental Hygiene school, my self-esteem had taken a beating. It's no surprise that my mini badass wanted to hide away, inside, afraid to stick her neck out again. I can't blame her for her fear.

I mean, look at what might happen if she did stand up for herself: even more rejection, more isolation, even more ignoring by me on the outside and the people who "love" me, because I was *just a girl.*

# CHAPTER 7

## *Getting Married*

I think I just *assumed the position*. As a girl I should get married, have some kids, and be there for my husband, so that's exactly what I did, though I didn't know that's what I was doing at the time. I met Gary during college at a Saint Louis University party. Neither of us went there; we both went with some friends. When my friend Theresa and I got to the party, she took off with her boyfriend and I stayed by myself, which wasn't a very safe thing to do. But it was always easy for me to socialize so I was fine. Eventually she came back. Then we walked all the way to the car, which was pretty for away, and I looked at her and said, "I think I want to go back and party with you now." I had spent the whole night, dancing, drinking, flirting and doing beer bongs all by myself, and I wanted to have some fun with her.

So we tracked all the way back to the party and Gary claims when he saw us coming into the party, we were laughing coming down the steps, and apparently he and his friend decided which one they would go for. Gary thought I was cute and started talking to me. We chatted, made out a little bit and then we had to go. He asked me for my number and I said, "No that's ok, no one ever calls me anyway. Don't worry about it." But he was insistent, and he followed us back to the car. I guess my kiss was pretty powerful. I still didn't give him my number, but Theresa wrote it on his hand just to stop him from asking!

He called me the next day after he was in the shower and noticed a number on his hand. Really? He had forgotten about my kiss? Wasn't he dreaming about me all night? No, he probably was too drunk and forgot all about me, so when he noticed he decided to get out of the shower to call me before it rinsed off. Otherwise, how would he know who'd given him her number?

We dated for three years, and I fell in love with Gary because he was such a big dreamer. His energy and excitement for life was contagious (occasionally it can be annoying). He was in maintenance at the time, going to HVAC school and he was confident that he would be able to move up at his company.

I definitely did not marry Gary for his money, like my Dad wanted. We actually both came into the marriage with the same amount. He treated me really well and I saw how he treated his mom and I knew he would be a really good husband and father. We dated three years before he proposed, nothing romantic mind you, it was after a fight we had had and he put the ring in some flowers and came over to the house. Yes, he proposed to me in my living room. *Soooo romantic* (can you hear the irony dripping from my lips?). I still give him trouble for that.

Now Gary was not my Dad's top choice for me. He assumed I would have married a dentist. He was always telling me to marry the first time for money, get divorced, and then marry for love. Gary did not have a lot of money and I am sure that was a concern for my father. He certainly did not want to put any more money out on me. He wanted me to be taken care of, like any good father would want.

Or maybe it was from the first time that they met. Gary came to pick me up, came into the house, and my Dad was coming down the steps at the same time. Yes, he had his blue jean shorts on, no shirt, and he had a Band-Aid on his nipple. Gary was probably nervous, or just stupid, and he said to my Dad, who he is meeting for the first time, "Hey, did you cut yourself shaving?"

Dad replied, "Who is this jerk?"

I said, "This is my date, Gary," and we ran out as fast as we could. We continued to date, and I kept bringing him back to the house but it wasn't easy for him. My family eventually grew to like Gary, probably because he was so entertaining and an easy mark for them to make fun of. And you know my family just loves to tease everyone. Turns out, we never did find out why he had a band aid on his nipple. I was always too afraid to bring it up again!

So, when I showed the ring to my Dad and told him Gary proposed, he answered back, "Good luck with that."

I replied with a few choice words that truly expressed how I felt, too. Words like, "You're an asshole," "I hate you!", "You're so mean," and probably a "Fuck you!" too. And I ran out. Again.

I went to the mall to meet my girlfriends to tell them the exciting news. We were having lunch and my mom and little brother Sean came up and handed me a note:

*Kelly,*

*I love you too much to hurt you. There are not enough words in the dictionary to say I am sorry. Please forgive me. You took it the wrong way. I like Gary. It's just you shouldn't surprise Archie Bunker when he wakes up after working all night. HaHa,*
    *Good Luck, Love Dad*

Since my family never stayed mad at each other very long, we acted like nothing ever happened, and went on with the wedding plans. I know a lot of families lacked communication skills back in the day, no one ever really talked about their feelings. I was definitely afraid I would get made fun of if I shared my feelings so I just acted like nothing bothered me, and that can make you a little bit of a hard ass for sure.

So Gary and I bought a house, about a mile away from my parents. It was a shit hole, but we spent six months getting it ready before we got married and moved in.

While we were working on the house, we were also planning a wedding. Correction: *I* was planning a wedding. My Mom and Dad gave me five thousand dollars to put towards the wedding, but my Dad mentioned there was a ladder on the side of the house also if I wanted to use that instead to run away. Yeah right, like he would have missed the time of his life. No one had more fun at my wedding than my

*Mom and Dad*

31

father, he had his buddy Teddy Cole as the DJ and I think my Mom and Dad danced all night. He even did his own dance to The King of Beer theme with his big beer belly sticking out. He was damn proud of his belly. He used to tell us how many years it took him to get that!

*Whose wedding was it anyway? Always the center of attention. And there I am, in the background. Like always.*

My Dad having his own solo dance at my wedding was not unusual, just typical for him to be center of attention. We all had a blast, the standard south side wedding with the buffet of roast beef, salad, green beans and of course mostaccioli. We danced all night and went through many kegs of beer since there were over five hundred people there. I honestly cannot tell you how many times Dad watched himself on my wedding video. However, I *can* tell you he watched it way more than I ever will.

If I could I would insert the video of Mom and Dad giving me a little speech on my wedding day. It was the two of them standing there wishing me all the best. Dad started out, "Kel, you witchy bitch, you're always cursing me out."

Mom elbowed him in the side and said, "Be nice!"

"Alright, Kel, I hope you and Gary are as happy as your mom and I after thirty years, and argue every day and then say you are sorry. Joan always says she is sorry!" *That man!*

So, this is the background of how I became whom I was in my twenties, thirties and forties. I was moving straight from a household of male dominance to living with one man. And I thought my role as a wife was to support any and all of my husband's dreams, because I was *just a girl*. I was so disconnected from whom I truly was or what I truly desired, I was not listening to my soul's desire to be uncovered. I didn't even know I had the right to follow my passion to help others. I was married and I was supposed to support Gary and build a life together, because that's how everyone else was doing it.

Along the way Gary became one of Dad's favorite people. He came to love Gary and just thought he was the best guy because he could fix anything. Plus they loved to watch the Discovery Channel on Sundays. We used to get phone calls from my Dad on Sundays telling us Mom was cooking and we should stop by. He just loved having us over.

Those were some great memories: hanging out on the deck, swimming in the pool, and of course playing washers for money. You know the game, you have partners, just like in horseshoes, but instead you have two square boxes with a coffee can in the middle, and you get points for throwing washers in the can, in the box and on the box.

*In the back yard, playing washers. Of course Dad wins every time.*

(I don't like the new plastic sets, you don't get that infamous sound from getting a washer in the can.) You couldn't play unless you had your dollar (my Dad was a betting man), and he loved to take people's money in everything he played. Horseshoes, washers, cards, shuffle board, golf, and I don't care what it was, he had a tendency to win a lot.

Now that I think about it, Dad never doubted himself when it came to winning. He had the right mindset and always a roll of cash in his pocket. He was just going to win every time, and he knew it!

33

So I did it, just the way I was taught. Get a job, find a man, get married, and buy a house. Check, check, check, and check! The only thing that I didn't do right away was have kids and everyone seemed ok with that. Now that I think about it, I wonder if not having kids was my way of controlling something, anything, because I could. Or maybe it was another way of trying to say, *I can live my life the way I want too.*

We lived about a mile away from my parents. We practically lived in the same neighborhood, shopped at the same stores, went to the same restaurants, and I at least tried to make the same meals. It was like we were conditioned to live very similar lives. You know when you are living in such a narrowly-focused world sometimes you will start living the same way, doing the same things, and even raising your kids the same way, but there are so many other ways to live your life. There are so many other things to see and to experience. You just have to decide to step into what you truly desire and actually start living the way you want.

# CHAPTER 8

*People Pleaser*

J ust like my mother, I became this people-pleasing woman to make sure people liked me, because I had such a high view of myself – *NOT!* – and I also made sure I was doing my share of the work load to make myself feel valuable. This seemed to be one of the major shifts in my life. Before, I had big plans: I was going to work part time as a dental hygienist, bartend on the weekends, get an apartment of my own, have some fun and find out who the hell I was. (I am laughing at myself right now - such big dreams!)

Instead, I got married and never had that all-important time to really discover what I really wanted to do with my life. I never had that time living with a girlfriend, dating whomever I wanted and staying up to all hours having those deep conversations. I missed just getting stupid crazy drunk and not giving a shit what people thought. I could have had more heartache and learned from it, I could have had more freedom and not have felt so trapped later on in life. I think I may have missed out on some experiences that may have helped me grow as a young woman. But then I wouldn't be writing this book.

I think I had that old programming installed in me that I was now operating from, a belief system that was injected slowly but surely over twenty years. The conditioning from everyone in my life was that girls are supposed to be supportive and make everyone around them happy, so I became a people pleaser. I know now that I was doing this to get people to like me.

I was always trying to impress my Mom and Dad to get their attention and their love because it wasn't shown a lot, so this became a part of my personality. I did what made others happy. I put my happiness to the side and my mini badass was slowly dying inside.

35

Being married to Gary has never been dull, never. That man has a lot of energy, a lot of gusto. My brother's favorite story about Gary is from when we were rehabbing our old house in the city. Gary went downstairs to the basement to grab a tool, and he noticed the steps were bad. So right then and there he tore them down and rebuilt them on the way back up. I think there might be a little ADHA going on there.

Gary had big dreams and I got caught up in everything he wanted to do, I found it exciting. I had never been around someone who had such energy and excitement for life, so it was new and kind of exhilarating. Since Gary was in Amway when we got married, we continued in that along with me working six days a week as a dental hygienist and Gary working full time plus some carpenter jobs on the side, and always doing something on that old house of ours. Boy did we have a lot of energy. I miss those days!

And the way Gary talked about it, I just knew we were going to be millionaires with Amway, but that never happened. I don't even think we made enough money to pay a bill. But that didn't stop us from trying other multi-level marketing businesses. Gary always had a way of convincing me that this was our way out of working our asses off. So along came Vaxa and ACN, which we never made money with either. Pretty sure we spent a lot more than we made. I told Gary never to come to me with another business opportunity. I was just fine working, no more *extras!*

After living in the city for eight years, putting about twenty-five thousand dollars into rehabbing our home, and having it on the market to sell for a year and a half, we finally got a buyer. But there was a catch: we had to loan the buyers five thousand dollars to help them purchase it. We were desperate, because we had found our dream home and we were ready to move, so we made the deal. In order to make it all work out, my parents loaned us the money to be able to loan the new buyers the money. Luckily, they were good people and paid us back every dime. Five years later, my Mom didn't want the money back, (Dad had passed by then) so we installed air conditioning in her house instead. I mentioned earlier that we didn't have air conditioning in our house, just a lot of fans. Dad always said we had a cool breeze coming in from the Mississippi River two blocks away, that AC wasn't necessary, and to jump in the pool if we were hot. So to be able to give my mom air conditioning for the first time felt like a real good thing to do.

We were so excited to get into our new home. It was perfect for us, perfect for two people who wanted to tear something up and make it their own, *and it already had air conditioning*. But boy, did it need some tearing up. It had ugly brown shag carpet everywhere, paneling on the walls, accordion doors, wallpaper on ceilings, orange carpet on the bathroom walls, brown and green toilets and gutters above the window to hold the lighting. And of course, green Astro Turf on the concrete outside in the back. We *loved* it. We tore that place up and continue to update it constantly. It's what we do.

But after being in the new house for five months, Gary decided he could no longer take the anxiety that his job was causing. He would tell me that when he crossed the Mississippi river every morning to go to Illinois to work on the pipeline for the Mississippi River Transmission Corporation (MRTC), his chest would get tight and he would have trouble breathing. So when he walked in one day and they were asking for volunteers to be let go and take a severance package, he couldn't raise his hand fast enough. He then called me after making that huge decision, all on his own, and told me what he had quit his job and was having a beer and a cigar with his buddy. I told him, "That's great honey, I will be here working."

I think I was still working six days a week at different dental offices. We needed as much money as possible after buying a house with a mortgage that was double compared to our old mortgage. Gary, on the other hand, was trying different career options. Since MRTC gave him a severance he was able to take some time and try different things.

One of them was insurance, but he couldn't pass the test. I still remember him pulling up and I could see it on his face when he didn't pass it for the third time. I simply said, "Baby, this might not be what you are supposed to be doing. What do you love to do? What are you really good at?"

He said, "I love to tear things up and put them back together. I love working with my hands." He had been doing side work on homes for years to make extra money, plus it was like our house was always under construction, and I thought it was the perfect time to try and start a business. He thought it would be too hard to have his own business, because other contractors had told him how hard it is to keep it going all year round. I told him, "Who cares what they say? This is your time, let's do it."

So we got a work truck, sent out letters to his old customers and everyone we knew, and we have been going steady for twenty three years. It has not always been easy running our own business, but when you focus on what you want and not the slow times, you can do anything. That is something I have been working on with Gary for years! He tends to freak out every time work slows down, not particularly because we won't make money, but he worries about the guys that work for us and their bills.

January tends to be our slow time and instead of Gary sitting around thinking about the work not coming in, I tell him to take a vacation with his buddies. It's a perfect time to get away and not think about work. I tell him to enjoy the time off and think about that phone ringing off the hook and more work than he can handle coming in, and when he takes that time off, things always change. Always.

Because that's what I had been doing for the first 30 years of my life, making sure everyone was happy and had all their needs taken care of. It almost felt like, if everyone else was happy then I was happy. But that is not how it works. Taking care of yourself is not selfish, trust me, being a people pleaser was a practice of mine that almost took me out.

# CHAPTER 9

*Losing My Dad*

S o there I was in my early thirties, working six days a week as a
hygienist, helping Gary build his construction business, plus there
was always a project going on in the new house. I remember going to the
home show one Saturday, Gary dragging my ass through that entire
convention center, looking at everything and talking to everyone. I was
mentally drained. We got there early in the morning and got home late
that evening. I had such a severe headache from the fluorescent lighting,
I couldn't wait to get my jammies on, take some Motrin and hit the couch.
I was done.

Then the doorbell rang, and I told Gary to get it, because I didn't have
a bra on (that's the very first thing I do when I get home, remove that
torture device) so he did and then he said it was a police officer and he
had some questions for us. So I got up, put a pillow in front of my chest
and went to the front door.

He opened it up a little more and there were about thirty five people
on my front lawn yelling, "SURPRISE!" Yes Gary and my brothers threw
me a surprise party that night. Now, I am just thinking, maybe it wasn't
such a good idea to drag my ass around the entire convention center,
knowing I was going to be partying all night. *Helloooooooo?* Anyway, the
Motrin kicked in, I did some shots and went on to have one of the best
nights ever. I remember my parents were there, and this would be the
last birthday party my Dad would be able to celebrate with me.

I found out the next week that he had lung cancer. No one thought it
was going to be as bad as it was. The doctors saw this little spot on his
lung when he had x-rays taken before his knee surgery several years
before and the doctor said it was nothing. Well, turns out, it was
*something.* Asshole. Dad went through the chemo treatments, and I

remember he was probably the only patient who wheeled his chemo bag outside to have a smoke. The man was not afraid, he just kept on going.

He also had surgery to try and remove the mass, but the doctor said it didn't look good and he may not have long to live. That was one of the worst days of my life. I'll never forget it.

He came home and Saint Joan earned another halo. She took care of the man like no one could. He even had her paged over the intercom at the hospital when he would go in for treatment. "Will Saint Joan please come to room 317, Saint Joan to Room 317." They truly loved each other.

That year we all spent as much time with him as we could. Luckily I didn't have kids yet, so I would go to the hospital at night whenever he was there to give Mom a break, and of course, my brothers were always there too. To be honest, I think we all did a lot of healing that year, because that time with Dad was incredible. It was the man we all loved without the alcohol, he was the sober Archie Bunker and we loved on him. I was there one night at home when we were trying to get him up in bed. His legs were so swollen he could barely walk, and it was extremely hard to get him up those stairs. So Mom was in front of him and I was behind him holding on and he said, "Well, this is probably the last time I will walk up these stairs." And he looked at Mom and said, "Is Kelly crying yet?" Remember, he loved to see me cry. And you know what, it *was* the last time he walked up those damn steps.

We lost him on April 29, 1997, and we threw one of the best damn Irish wakes you have ever seen, partly due to the fact that Dad insisted on it. He used to tell us that he saved money in his pockets for his party and we knew exactly what he meant, but we never talked about it until he passed. And when we went to check his pockets, we found over seven hundred dollars and we knew exactly what he wanted us to do with it: buy beer.

And buy beer we did. We spent every dime and brought it all into the Southern Funeral Parlor. I don't recall how many people came to the funeral, but the parking lot was packed with open trunks and a lot of drinking going on both outside and inside. People would walk in and no one was in the parlor where Dad was, because we were all in the basement drinking, doing it the Southside Irish way. He would have been so proud.

It is still hard to think about him not being here, especially when my daughters say, "I think Papa would have really liked me." My oldest daughter Maggie even wears a shirt to bed that has PAPA on it. That is the hardest thing for me, that my Dad never got to see my beautiful girls. I believe he sees them from the other side, but it's not the same. Just thinking about it makes me cry, you can imagine the tears rolling down my face right now, and I know my Dad is loving it!

It may have not been easy growing up with my Dad some days, but his strong character, his great love for his family and for life itself made me the person I am today. I am a strong woman who can handle almost anything, when I am connected to my Inner Badass.

# CHAPTER 10

*Baby or No Baby?*

E veryone just assumes after you get married, you are supposed to get pregnant. Well that didn't interest me at all. I didn't even know if I would ever have a baby. Kids are a lot of responsibility. I knew this because I had spent so much time with my younger brothers. Don't get me wrong, I loved them, but they were a lot of work.

So, when I got married I knew what it took to care for a baby and had no desire to do that in my twenties. I was having too much fun rehabbing, partying, and traveling, plus Gary and I were working a lot, and that doesn't leave a lot of time to be with children. I truly believe that having that time alone with your spouse really helps you get to know each other. Throwing kids into the mix too early can add a lot of stress right away. There are a lot of adjustments when you get married and working through all those things really can help you handle anything.

So, when Gary and I were not working we spent our money on traveling, we went everywhere. We loved to ski, and we went to Colorado almost every year and went to all the different resorts. We also went to Tahoe, Germany, Austria and of course, our all-time favorite trip was to Ireland. That was our last trip over the pond before we had our first baby, Maggie.

People spent a lot of time wondering when I was going to have a baby. That must have thought it was odd to be married so long and not have kids. They would ask, "Are you pregnant yet?" "Are you guys ever going to get pregnant," "Are you guys having trouble getting pregnant?"

I would always reply, "Have you not met Gary yet?" He's got a ton of energy, and he never stops moving, and I think he has a little ADHA going on. He is constantly saying *Kel, Kel, Kel, Kel, Kel*. So if I would have kids, there would be a lot of, *Mom, Mom, Mom, Mom, Mom,* along with

*Kel, Kel, Kel, Kel, Kel,* not sure anyone could handle that. I wasn't quite sure I was ready for that, but if I decided to do it, I definitely wasn't going to have them two years apart like everyone else was doing. That looked like too much chaos!

But after ten years into it, we were at my cousin's farm, all sitting around the bonfire drinking. I had this vision, swear to God, that I was going to have two kids. I told Gary and he said, "Oh, should I go get the tent up?" The man thought I wanted to do it at my cousin's farm!

I said, "No, we have to go to Ireland first, because once we have them we won't be able to go." You see, I was lucky enough to be born on Saint Patrick's Day and I just love being part of an Irish Clan, so going over to Ireland had been a dream of mine forever. As usual he thought I was crazy, but I came home from the farm and bought two airline tickets right away. Unfortunately, we had to put it off for five months because Gary's mom had lung cancer and we were afraid to go right away because it didn't look good for her.

Sad to say she died a week before we were to leave, but it turned out to be a relief for us because she was suffering and we didn't have to worry about her on the trip. So, we went to Ireland, traveled all over, never knowing where we were going to stay. We always found little bed and breakfasts to stay at and had *the most amazing trip* of our lives.

We went from town to town and hung out with the people. We stayed at their homes and went to their taverns, and I really got to understand why my Irish family is a little crazy. The Irish just like to have fun and tell stories, and not all the stories are true, but they know how to tell a good one.

One of the funniest things that happened to us in Ireland was when we were going see the Skellig Michael Island off the west coast of Ireland. We had boarded a boat with ten other passengers and we were excited for the eight mile ride out to the islands where the monks built beehive-shaped homes to hide out from the Vikings. So we were on the boat, and as usual Gary was talking to the captain. (Did I mention that Gary talks to everyone he sees? We'll even be out to dinner and he starts talking to the table next to us. It can be a little irritating.) So he was talking and the captain asked him if he knows how to drive a boat, and Gary

"Captain" Gary

Visiting the Skellig Michaels of Ireland

said of course. Then the guy proceeded to tell Gary that he was filling in for his brother who couldn't make it in that morning because he may have had too many Guinness beers the night before. But then the captain thought he may have had too many Guinness himself and needed to pass out in the sleeping quarters.

Well Gary thought that was fantastic and he said, "Yes, I can do that." And all of a sudden we had a new skipper on the boat. The captain told Gary to wake him up when we got close to the island. Meanwhile, the other passengers were wondering what's going on, and I was actually telling them that Gary was friends with the captain and was helping him out while the captain went below to work on something. No need to mention the hangover. The passengers were cool with it, and that's the Irish for you, they are pretty laid back over there.

So we survived the boat trip, traveled around Ireland a couple more days, flew over to London while we were there, checked out that city and then finally came back home after two fun-filled weeks. And I am so glad we took that time to relax and have fun, because a month later we got pregnant. The party was officially over. We had our little Maggie Joan Kimberlin on April 7, 2000, twelve years after we got married. She definitely was not in a hurry to get out. That little stinker had me in labor for 24 hours. She waited until Friday night, party night, which explains her personality a little bit. She is my social bug.

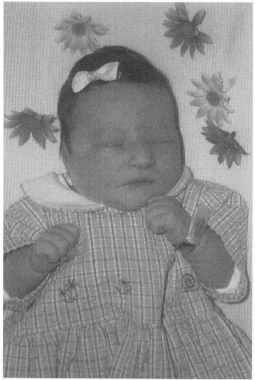

*Maggie Joan*

And I remember the cord was around her neck. They had to take her away to make sure she would start breathing and while they were doing that, I was throwing up, my whole body hurt and I was completely exhausted. I had worked up until the day I gave birth. I had the hemorrhoids to prove it. So when they handed Maggie to me, and told me to try and breast feed her, I told them they could do that for me, I was fucking tired and I will be feeding her the rest of her life, you can do it for the first twenty four hours, because I need to sleep. I am sure they thought I was crazy.

I was, and it only continued to get worse. I came home, had six weeks off work to spend with Maggie, but something was off. My milk wouldn't come in, so I couldn't breast feed. (I wasn't too upset about that.) I couldn't sleep, I was extremely irritable, more than usual, I was losing my hair, I was gaining more weight, I had brain fog, I was constipated, which lead to more hemorrhoids and I didn't want anything to do with Maggie. Maybe I was right about not having a baby, this fucking sucks!

I thought I had postpartum depression. I called my mother and said, "Why didn't you warn me about this? I don't understand what is going on."

She replied, "Don't you have some friends to call? I don't know what to do." Yikes, I guess I freaked her out a little. She wasn't the only one. I remember going into the closet at work and crying in between patients, because I felt like shit. I did call my friends but no one had experienced the kind of symptoms I was having.

Then one day, I got on the phone with my girlfriend Stathy (yes, that is spelled right, she's Greek), and told her how I was feeling and she said, "Kel, have you had your thyroid checked? I have a girlfriend that had the same symptoms and her thyroid was not working. Go check that out with your doctor." So I did, and that was exactly the problem. My thyroid was completely shut down. No wonder I felt like shit, it was so nice to know that it wasn't just me feeling crazy, that there was actually something wrong with my body.

This baby thing was hard, but after I got medication for the thyroid issues, I went to just being like all the other new moms. I now only had the symptom of complete exhaustion, but I knew that was normal and temporary, and that I was in love with my little monkey again. Life was back to crazy normal. Crazy normal I can handle, so after a couple years we decided we would try for a second baby. Remember, I didn't want them two years apart, I always said three. So on April 7 again, this time 2003, our little Brooke Ann Kimberlin came along. Exactly three years later. That's what happens when you "schedule" sex!

Now Brooke was born on a Monday, which explains why they can have the same birthday and can be so different. She looked exactly like Maggie though, with the same curly black hair, which scared the hell out of me both times. I just thought I would have bald babies, and they both came out with massive sets of hair and big blue eyes and just a couple ounces different in weight. It definitely was like déjà vu.

Except for the fact that Gary almost missed Brooke's birth. We didn't have time to bring Maggie to the babysitter and then go to the hospital,

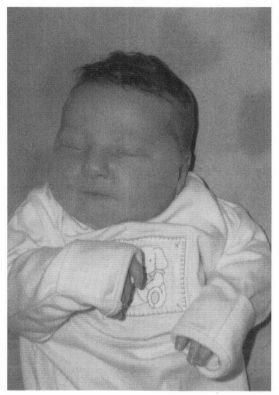

*Brooke Ann*

so I drove myself, and Gary dropped Maggie off. I went into the hospital, just barely dilated and I was carrying *everything I needed,* because I was afraid Gary would forget something. I had a pillow, overnight bag, purse and a camera case. I told the lady I was in labor and she kept looking around me to see who was with me, and I told her *It's just me, let's get this going.*

After the second epidural, because the first one didn't work, and they are so amazingly fun to get, I couldn't wait to get another one, I was dilating pretty fast and Gary was nowhere to be found, which was surprising, because remember, he gets excited about everything. So I called him,. He picked up the phone, and I said in my normal *I am going to kick your ass* tone, "Where the hell are you?"

He said, in his excited voice, "You won't believe who I ran into at the gas station?"

"You're fucking right, I won't believe it," I said. "I don't care to ever fucking know who you ran into, but I will tell you one thing. If you miss the delivery of this baby, don't bother stepping into the room!" Luckily, he made it, but I think it was just minutes before I delivered another mini Gary. He is the one with the cold black curls by the way. I still don't know who he ran into that day.

So that was it, two babies three years apart and I only had six weeks off of work again, so we took the girls to Florida on a plane. Brooke was only four weeks old, but she was perfect. It was the crazy three year old that decided to jump right into the pool and teach herself how to swim. She's been swimming ever since. And even though I was in no frame of mind to buy anything, while we were down there we also went on one of those crazy time share tours. And guess what? Gary worked his magic on me once more and by the time we left we were the proud owners of a new time share condo. Oh joy.

My milk did come in this time and I was able to breastfeed Brooke (oh joy). This was not the most exciting or bonding thing I have ever done, like some people tell you. Nope, I had the blisters and bleeding of the nipples and I never had enough, or it seemed like that.

I had the problem of trying to get Brooke to drink from a bottle because she was like a beast at the breast and there was never enough for her. In fact, she's still like that, a huge eater and yet still skin and bones. She gets that high metabolism from her Daddy, not her Momma. So there I was trying to get back to work and Brooke wouldn't let anybody else feed her. I actually left her at the neighbors with a bottle and she refused it for hours.

Eventually I had to recruit my neighbor Craig, who had four babies of his own. I really thought if anyone could get her to drink from a bottle, it would be him. He was also the one who nicknamed her Brooklyn. God rest your soul Craig, you were a good man. But he couldn't get her to take a bottle either, so I had to go back to work and bring the little nipple biter with me, and nurse her in between patients. The fun never stops with children, or husbands, if you choose to keep them!

*So glad I did!*

# CHAPTER 11

*The Shit Show Continues*

G ary had met someone who said he would like to work with us to add roofing to our business, and that I could do all the insurance paperwork that came along with it. Gary thought that would add income to our Kimberlin Construction business, so we decided that it would be a good time for me to quit dental hygiene. So we went into business with the new guy.

As it turns out, this guy was actually stealing clients and information from his prior boss. We had no idea until we were served papers that we were being sued. Isn't life fun? So imagine this situation, I had just given birth, couldn't get my baby to take a bottle, quit my steady job and had big dreams to work together with my husband to build up our own business, and suddenly we might lose *everything* because someone has decided to sue us. I cannot tell you how high the tension and anxiety were in our house.

I was still hormonal and simply wanted to kill Gary for getting us in this situation, and for his part, he was devastated that he did this to his family. We decided to meet the old boss, Bill, in a Walgreen's parking lot and talk to him about what the hell was going on. Luckily he was a really nice guy. He explained to us that his ex-employee was sneaking into the office and taking his clients' info, and then using that to poach those clients away from him. He assumed we were part of it, but we were able to convince him we weren't. The crazy thing is, we became friends with Bill and worked with him for years doing roofing. Gary actually goes on cigar trips with Bill occasionally and we have remained good friends over the years.

So, this anxiety which usually turns into resentment with me was slowly affecting my body and I didn't know it. Any toxic emotion you keep in your body affects your cells and this was just the beginning. My cells didn't know what the hell was going on. There was so much toxicity in my body it was starting to take a toll, and I didn't even know it was happening. But I did know that I did not have the patience to love Gary through this shit. Instead of killing him, or finding a safe way to express my feelings, I held on to a lot of negative emotions. Later on I came to find out that holding on to negative, resentful, angry feelings can really affect your health. I'll show you all the consequences of this in my life later.

Construction was never enough for Gary. He was always looking for ways to make more money, especially since I quit my job to help him build his business. We lost my income and had to replace it. On the plus side, it was great to be home with the kids part time. Moms that are home full time are saints, there is no other way to put it. Hardest job on the planet.

So there we were building our business and Gary started buying homes to rehab and either sell or keep for rentals. We bought one in University City, Missouri, and that flipped really well. We made money after adding an entire livable second story. Then we bought three more in South county and started renting those out and all of a sudden I was a landlord. Not my favorite thing in the world.

I'm too nice when it comes to collecting rent when people are having money issues. I really don't like to knock someone down during hard times. That's why you should hire a property manager, but I thought I needed to do everything to earn my keep. WTF! But that's who I was. If I wasn't working twelve to fourteen hours a day then I thought I wasn't good enough. When you get to that state of mind, you're really fucked in the head.

Ultimately, this would be another thing that was affecting my health, not feeling worthy enough, thinking I wasn't good enough, that Gary wouldn't love me if I didn't do my share. Looking back, I was doing the work of three people. Most women usually are. We think we are only worthy and of value when we are working our asses off, and we beat ourselves up when we think we aren't earning our keep. I was the queen of beating the shit out of myself. My insides were black and blue from all the self-abuse. You know when that internal critic tells you you're not good enough, you're a piece of shit, you don't deserve anything, you suck at being a parent, no one likes you. Sound familiar? That bullshit did nothing but put me on the fast track to my breakdown.

Gary got the idea one day that Benton Park would be the next up and coming area in St. Louis. So he bought three historical homes that were completely gutted, down to the studs. I'm pretty sure my name was *not* on those properties. He was probably afraid to show them to me because I would have said, *Oh, hell no! We ain't buying those houses.* One was actually leaning and the other was a shell, maybe just one bedroom, and the third one was a total piece of shit. But they were "historical" and that meant we would get credit and money back on anything we restored. Unfortunately, it also meant that someone had to keep track of every penny we spent on them, on certain forms and had to be turned in on a timely manner. And who's going to do that? Oh, okay, I guess I didn't have anything else going on, bring it on.

We were rehabbing two of them at the same time, which got a little crazy, and this happened in 2008! Good memories, 2008. A lot of people lost everything during the market crash, but we kept going, took huge construction loans, finished the rehabs and rented those houses out. We never finished the third. All of a sudden I was managing five houses, running a construction business, taking care of the girls, my own home, managing to keep the dogs alive and anything else that came up. And then, what do you know? Something *else* popped up on Gary's radar, a garage door business that some friends wanted us to invest in. Sure, why not, Kelly's not that busy!

Fast forward, maybe four months later, I found myself at Loughborough and Broadway trying to run a garage door business on top of all the other shit I was taking care of. I would have my girls down there occasionally with our partners' kids and they were chasing rats as big as cats in the warehouse. What the hell were we thinking? Our partners convinced us that this was a great location and the perfect timing to open a warehouse because there wasn't much competition. That was until another company opened two weeks after we did, with a following already *and* a better location. And probably fewer rats!

I was really starting to lose it. I had to have a loaded gun in my drawer just in case. On top of that I had to wear long underwear and a parka every day so I wouldn't freeze my ass off. Yeah, my life just kept getting better and better. I decided to put my daughter into a full time daycare, because that was not the place to keep her all day.

Finally, two years into "Hell on Broadway," I told Gary to get me the hell out of there or I was leaving him, I was that desperate. I wanted out of that place, but our partners weren't budging. They wanted to stay and we couldn't just shut it down. I would have tried anything to get the hell out of there. I invited a Feng Shui practitioner down there to try and shift the energy so someone could buy us out but that didn't work either. I even pulled my father into it.

I spent a lot of afternoons at Jefferson Barracks National Cemetery having a beer with my Dad. He was the only one listening to me at that time in my life. I would get a couple beers, drive over there, and just pulling in that beautiful military cemetery made me feel better, it was majestic. I would grab a blanket, my little cooler of beer and walk to his headstone and just lean on it for hours. I remember my heart just aching, wishing I could really talk to him. I was in a lot of emotional pain and didn't understand why my life seemed so chaotic, or what the hell I was doing wrong. I needed all the help I could get and I assumed he had some pull up there in Heaven.

Luckily, and possibly due to the three protection rocks I put behind the building (it's a Feng Shui thing), we were bought out by the owner of the warehouse. Thank God, he saved us and our marriage, but it ain't over yet. You might want to get a drink ready for what's coming next.

# CHAPTER 12

*Gary Takes His Turn Falling Apart*

G etting out of that garage door business made being a landlord seem like high society work. I was so fucking happy to be back at my home office, no gun or parka needed there, and I could be home to get the girls off the bus. Things were going pretty smoothly. We had the income properties, Kimberlin Construction was growing (in fact, we hired another salesman and four more carpenters), and I was OK with more paperwork and dealing with all the interesting tenants. Hell, that could be another whole book. Lord did I hear some stories.

So, we were cruising in Kimberlin Construction, were able to do a lot of work on our own home, did some traveling and then the shit hit the fan. Our new salesman had a huge $100,000 job that wasn't bid right. He set it up so that there was NO PROFIT on it. We worked on that job for six months, and when you are a small company, six months without profit can take you out. I think we had about two thousand dollars in the account and a lot of bills to pay, so we had to let our salesman go. We just couldn't afford any more mistakes.

To compound the problem, some of the carpenters left because they came with the salesman. That was OK with us, because we decided bigger wasn't better, just more headaches. More workman's comp insurance, more liability, more medical insurance, more payroll, more schedules, more overtime, more everything. It was a lot to cover and we were not in a place to cover it.

But we regrouped and decided we were good with the amazing guys we'd had for years. I call them the good old boys. We can trust them, they always do the right thing and our customers love them.

Funny side story, as usual. We were at the wedding of one of the newer guys, and a lot of his buddies from the company he used to work for were sitting at our table. They didn't know who we were. So, I was talking to one of them and ask them how they know the groom, and he says they used to work with each other. "And as a matter of fact," this friend said, "he's thinking about quitting where he was and coming to work with us again."

I said, "That's great." We get up to visit the buffet and the friend said, "So how do you know Ryan?"

I looked right at him, so I could see his face when I said, "He works for me." He looked like he saw a ghost, not knowing what to say, he just kept apologizing and I just kept laughing, it was hysterical. Absolutely priceless. We really didn't care, we were always fine when someone needed to leave and move on to something else. That is one of my favorite stories; it still makes me laugh, and *laughter* has gotten me through all the tough stuff in my life.

Again, things were going fairly smoothly for having our own business. I mean there was always something to deal with, like one of our guys falling off a roof and catching his leg on the ladder and snapping it in half, or another guy trying to sell marijuana to a customer, or when we had to tell someone to go home because he was still drunk from the night before. Just to be clear, none of those guys work for us anymore. We are a reputable company with our good old boys still employed and happy to show up for work. And show up sober!

But I think the pressure was getting to Gary and he started having anxiety attacks. He often thought he was dying. We were at a friend's lake house one weekend and he thought he was having a heart attack. He even told me to get the girls so he could say goodbye and tell them he loved them. I did, after he asked several times, because I knew he was having an anxiety attack and I was trying to calm him down, but nothing was working.

He insisted we call an ambulance and we did. The paramedics came out to the deck, where he was saying his last words, checked him all out and told him everything was OK and he was probably having an anxiety attack, not a heart attack. *Finally*, I thought. *Someone else was saying it.* I think he thought that it was weak to have an anxiety attack and that a heart attack sounded more manly.

Even after the paramedics confirmed his heart was ok, he insisted having them drive them to the hospital. I offered, but he thought he would have a heart attack on the way there and he wanted to be in an ambulance, so they did. And I told him to call me when he was all checked out again and I would pick him up. There's nothing worse than sitting in a waiting room for someone to confirm you're just a hypochondriac. This wasn't his first visit to the emergency room.

So after several hours of him insisting that they do every test – every test - they confirmed that he has some anxiety and should take some medicine for it. Of course, he refused.

Two weeks later we were in Michigan, our favorite place to vacation and he looked at me and said, "Call an ambulance, I think I'm having a heart attack."

I said, "Gary, your heart is fine. I just paid thousands of dollars to get all those tests that aren't covered, and they said you have anxiety."

He said, "Are you going to call an ambulance or am I?" Maggie and Brooke were getting ready to go to the beach, and I didn't want to scare them, so I told them I would be right back and I drove Gary to the emergency room and dropped him off at the door. Because, once again, I was not going to wait to have them confirm, dozens of tests and thousands of dollars later, that he simply had anxiety.

Yet he insisted on getting every test again, to make sure the other ones were right. Three or four hours later I came back to pick him up. The doctors seemed to be laughing at me because I was the worst spouse ever, just dropping him off and picking him up, like a kid at the mall. At least I didn't make him take a cab home! That's pretty good for me.

So it came to pass that on top of everything else I had a hypochondriac husband to take care of, who refused to take medicine for his anxiety. Maybe if he did have a heart attack, he just might take his medicine. This became just another job to add to my list, taking care of my hypochondriac husband. I am always the one trying to calm him down when he gets overly excited about things, and he gets overly excited about a lot of things, a lot of little things, like tiny little things. I am so serious right now.

I tried everything. I let him put a pool table in the living room, let him buy a boat, encouraged him to go on guy trips (that was really for my sanity, too), and took on everything else besides bidding on jobs so he didn't spend any more money on useless tests.

You see, I don't have much sympathy for people who have been diagnosed and refuse to do anything about it, especially after my own excruciating back labor, hemorrhoids, sleep deprivation, pushing out two babies, and ruining my vajajay. To be honest, a little anxiety sounds like a vacation.

The stress was piling up on me and I began to think, *Every time we do something different I will be happier, more fulfilled.* But that was not the case. These were all Gary's ambitions, his dreams, and I just followed along because his excitement for any new adventure was admittedly a little contagious and I had nothing of my own going on. Plus I was still in this mindset that is was my job to make sure everyone around me was happy. It can be exhausting.

You are not going to believe this, but he actually convinced me to join another multi-level marketing business, again, called ACN. I thought it would take some pressure off of him to help with extra income. He told me we would be able to broker internet, phone and cable but also in some states, electric and gas were being deregulated and we would eventually be able to broker those utilities. He said we would be in the forefront of the utility sales. It sounded so amazing, even though, remember, I had told him to never ever come to me with another MLM business again. He had some balls and he convinced me to give it one last try.

We went to our first ACN convention in North Carolina on our 25th wedding anniversary. No, we were not at the beach, or the mountains, we were in Downtown Charlotte, to spend 2 days in a convention hall. Sooooo romantic. I know many of you are thinking, damn they're crazy, why do they keep doing all this stupid shit? The only thing I can come up with is that, for myself, I wanted to support Gary. I knew he wanted to take care of his family no matter what, and the construction business isn't always easy, so he was always looking to invest in something that he thought would help his family. He really is a good guy, I just like to make fun of him, because he's crazy too.

But for me, I had lost myself a long time ago. I knew I wanted to help people and since I got derailed from going into psychology, I thought my job was to support and help Gary with any and all adventures, no matter what. And, I admit, I thought a new adventure would fulfill my soul's purpose. I loved helping people have hope in building their own businesses and making their own money, but nothing was making me feel good about *myself.* Nothing.

Can you guess who got to run the ACN business, setting up the services and doing all the paperwork? Yep that would be me. Gary doesn't even know how to turn on a computer. He can build you a house, but God forbid he remembers what I showed him on the computer. To be fair, he actually is way smarter than I make him out to be. He's a clever man, just a little technologically impaired.

You know, I sometimes had people tell me that they had a "real job" and I didn't, and that I didn't understand how hard it was to work all week. You know, that's real funny, because I know people couldn't do in a week even half the shit I got done in one day! At that point in my life, a "real job" of 40 hours a week would have been a fucking picnic.

# CHAPTER 13

*Saint Joan Slowly Leaves Us*

J ust to add to the chaos, my Mom started showing signs of dementia. I noticed it first. My brothers didn't believe me, but I knew mom pretty well. The very first strange thing that I noticed (you might need another drink, a strong one at that), was when my mom had asked me to drive her to the doctor because it was snowing, and of course I said yes. Driving to the doctor was not the strange part.

We went, and I drove her, thinking it would just be a regular visit. The nurse came out and called me her into the room, though I was planning on relaxing in the waiting room and reading some gossip in the People magazine. The nurse looked directly at me. She said, "Are you the one who will be taking care of the wound?"

I looked around the room and asked, "Are you talking to me?" They said yes and invited me into the room with my mother. She proceeded to pull her pants down so they could check the spot where they had done a procedure to remove this god-awful staph infection on her butt cheek. And yet this is still not the strange part. Then they start inserting this long-ass Q-tip into the infection. I mean this motherfucker went *all* the way in, knuckle-deep. I almost threw up as they were giving me instructions to clean her ass cheek twice a day.

I said absolutely not. We would hire a nurse to do that before I get anywhere near her ass and a staph infection. Are you kidding me? Hell no. They went on to tell me I had to do it, nurses didn't come over for small things like this. My mother seemed like she was in La La Land. She was just like, oh well, we will figure it out. That was my first clue to just how far gone she was, when she didn't even comprehend how serious an infection she had in her second ass-hole!

In the end, there was no figuring it out. It was *all Kelly* again, the caretaker of everyone. The first time I went to her house after the doctor visit, my brother Brian was there for lunch, just like he always was. He would do the puzzle in the newspaper with my mom, make lunch and refresh his iced tea that she would always have ready. Did I mention he was my mom's favorite? All the way until the very end!

So he was there, and as I explained what happened at the doctor's office, he could not stop laughing. I told him *he* should do it, and he just laughed again. I took a shot of whiskey and started upstairs. Finally, here comes the weirdest part, my mom was naked, completely naked. My mom never walked around naked. She was very conservative, so to see that was a bit of a shock.

She was just not herself I could tell, I think this was the beginning of the end. Anyway, I told her I only had to see one butt cheek, which would be plenty, and asked her to put her clothes back on, please! I cleaned out the wound, just barely able to do it without gagging. When I went back downstairs, Brian had left, but before he did he'd gotten out all the liquor in the house and put it on the table with a note for me: *Have at it Kel!* And I did. That was one long week of drinking and pus swabbing.

Seeing my Dad die was easy compared to watching my mother, who had only given of herself her whole life, slowly succumb to dementia. She did not deserve to die like that. The next seven years were torture, to put it mildly. We had to take her money away, take her car away (that was a fun night), and then try to clean out her house when she wasn't looking. Some of the people who get dementia become hoarders and she was one of them. She had so much Tupperware, glassware, and a shit load of clothes, because she kept buying the same things over and over again.

I also had the privilege of taking her to the grocery store since we took her car away, and it was so stressful. She would scream and yell and throw the things out of the cart. You would have thought I was abusing her by the way she was carried on. So I stopped that after a few times. I was just trying to get her out of the house for a bit.

We kept her at her house for about two years, all doing our share of visiting, shopping and paying her bills, and just waiting for the signs to say, *Ok, now is the time*. Eventually we had to make the decision of where and when we should place her in a facility, and that just sucked. I remember going around looking at places and my stomach would just get so upset. I would see people just sitting in wheel chairs with that lost look on their face, or they would try and talk to me thinking that they knew me, it was not fun thinking that this would be the condition mom will eventually be in. I just couldn't believe that this was happening.

We waited and waited. Sean was in the house one day visiting and Mom let in a complete stranger, posing as a "Honey Do" kind of guy. Within minutes of talking to Mom he should have known that she could not have made any decisions about work on her house. She had lost her words but didn't know it, so she would insert "Just a minute" wherever she felt necessary. At the end of her speaking days it was all "Just a minute, just a minute." She could tell a whole story with those words and she thought she was telling you something. That poor woman. Needless to say, Sean asked the man to leave and that was it. I think we had her in a home the following week.

Luckily my brother Mick had found a place in Webster Groves that was in between all us, so we were able to put her in the Alzheimer's unit that following week. That was a good time. Trying to find a way to get my mom to go into assisted living was yet another shit show. We had Sean take her out to lunch like he did every Saturday and the rest of us went over to her house, packed the bed, the dresser, clothes, TV, knickknacks, and anything to make her new room seem like home to her. Well, home to somebody going into lock down. You should have seen the residents rush to the door to try and get out when we were carrying things in.

I remember the day we put her in there, obviously upset. So I told her, "Mom, you are surrounded by your loved ones and we just want you to be safe. This is your new home. We love you and we're sorry."

She got off of her couch, pointed her crooked, arthritic finger at me and managed to get out the words, "Not you, not you." So I guess this meant I didn't love her because I did all this to her. She blamed me for everything that happened. They say you blame the people closest to you. At least, that's what I was thinking in my head. That was a tough five years of visiting that facility. My brothers and I always talked about pushing that number three in the elevator and getting that twinge in your stomach every time we went to that third floor where all those sad souls were spending their last days. It was never easy.

I actually ran into a lady a couple months after my mom had passed and she asked if I was Joan's daughter and I said yes. She said, "I remember you at Provisions, my mom was on the same floor as your mom."

I said, "Oh I'm sorry I don't recall seeing you," and she told me that most times she saw me, I was upset and crying and she didn't want to disturb me. Those were some tough times and they are hard to remember and even harder to explain.

It was like my heart ached, for her and myself. Every time I went in to see her, it was like losing her all over again. The worst was when I would walk in and she'd be in her wheelchair looking out the window. That's when I usually lost it, I just imagined her sitting there asking herself *What the hell happened? Why am I here? Who am I? Why can't I speak or walk?* Then, when I would go talk to her and look into her eyes and see nothing, nothing, that was just one of the many parts we had to deal with.

It was emotionally draining for all of us, especially when we would think she was on her last breath and then she would bounce back. I can't remember how many people died in the time Mom lived there but it was a lot. We used to joke that the building would be on fire and somehow Mom would open the locked doors, find her way down to the first floor and wheel herself out the main door through all the smoke. There were so many people dying from pneumonia, the flu and heart attacks, and there was Mom, still sitting in her room with the dented drywall that she punched with her fist. That woman was stubborn.

I think we "lost" her about four times. At one point they called in hospice, because once again she was near the end. They were feeding her, rubbing her feet, playing the violin for her. Turned out they were stimulating her back to health! I was so pissed when I walked in and saw that I had to kick them out. She lived for another two and a half years, the longest two and a half years I ever experienced.

We lost her September 28, 2017, the day after her great-granddaughter arrived. My parents must like doing things around birthdays, because my father passed the day after my brother Mick's birthday. I won't go into too much detail, but if you ever saw anyone shrink to skin and bones and slowly stop breathing, it is one of the worst things I've ever been through. My brothers and I went there day and night that week, because we didn't want her to die alone and my poor brother Mick, who just had his first granddaughter Sophie the day before, ended up being the one that was with her when she passed. I was on my way over but I think they would have suspected something if I had been around. I did say I was going to suffocate her with a pillow many, many times. I should have been the first one they looked at if something suspicious happened. I just couldn't take her living like that, Mom was beautiful, and I hated seeing her mumbling her words, drooling on herself and wearing a diaper. She would have been so mad she ended up like that.

Mom's condition just added to the stress in my life. I felt the need to check on her all the time, so we knew she was being treated right, and let me tell you, those angels at Provisions treated Mom like a queen, even after the time she came at them swinging in the shower. I could always tell by the way she would smile at them when they walked into the room, unlike the snarl I would get every time I showed up. She hated me. I know it was the disease, but it still hurts inside.

And it hurts when you see your mother deteriorate right before your eyes, when she loses her voice, when she can no longer walk, when she forgets she is supposed to be mad at you. All of it, it all *sucks!* So this obviously was taking a toll on me too and added to the problems that had already started in my body.

# CHAPTER 14

*What the Hell Happened?*

I usually come across as a pretty tough cookie, definitely a badass, but I was slowly dying inside. I was not myself anymore. I would wake up every night in cold sweats (not hot flashes, that's the next book), worrying about renters moving out of the houses, having to come up with two or three mortgage payments at the same time, forgetting to pay bills, trying to broker services with our ACN business, taking care of Kimberlin Construction, taking care of all the houses, paying all those bills, paying all of our personal bills, paying all of Mom's bills, taking care of all the kid stuff, the house stuff and even the fucking dogs. It just blows my mind that no one else in the house knew if the dogs were ever fed or what day the trash was supposed to go out. My brain was on overload with every little thing, which drove my stress hormones to super-high levels.

Hormones can really send a sane person over the edge. My adrenals were working overtime, they usually just send out the cortisol hormone when you are in a fight or flight situation, like if you are being chased by a dog, or in a school yard fight with your lunchbox for a weapon. Then they stop sending the hormone out when you are finished running or settle down, but my adrenals were so fatigued, they were releasing cortisol all the time and I was a hot mess.

I noticed things were getting worse when a renter moved out and we had to go over and clean the house to get it ready to sell. I was working on the toilet and the tub, because people never bothered to do it and I thought to myself, *I am never going to clean someone else's toilet again.* Then Gary called me outside to help him clean the siding and the soffit and I stood on the ladder, thinking, *This is fucking stupid,* and he said, "Aren't you going to clean the fascia?"

I said, "That is not going to sell the house,"

He said, "Do you want to help or not?" Well you can probably guess what my answer was. *Hell no!* I was out of there.

So I went to the gas station, got two beers and drove to Jefferson Barracks Cemetery to have a drink with my Dad. I drove there knowing where he was buried, but when I was walking around to find him, I couldn't and I was just sobbing because I felt so alone, frustrated, lost, full of anger, resentful, you name any bad emotion, I felt it.

Some poor guy came up to me and asked if I needed help finding a headstone and I told him yes. He radioed it in and found my Dad right there in front of me. That's how out of it I was. I sat there for a couple hours, poured some beer over his stone, leaned on it like I usually did, drank my beer, and begged him to help me if he could. I couldn't take it anymore and I was desperate. I just felt like shit most days. I couldn't sleep, I was shaking all the time, I didn't have any energy, my muscles hurt *all the time*, I was exhausted, and depressed, and I had started getting anxious about everything.

I broke down a lot in the following days, and I started drinking earlier and earlier every day just to numb my pain and try to control my shaking. I didn't know anything back then about cortisol levels being out of whack but I felt like I was in flight or fight mode all the time. The worst part of this whole situation was that my daughters could see I was falling apart, and I am sure that was freaking them out, seeing their strong mama become weak. The guilt and the shame from them seeing me depressed and hiding in the basement most nights so they wouldn't see me cry and drinking all night made me feel even worse. The stress just kept piling on.

I thought I was stronger than this. I didn't feel like myself and I was scared. *Is this what the rest of my life is going to be like?* I wondered. *Will I ever start to feel better? How come I can't handle anything calmly? Why does my world look like it's falling apart? What kind of example am I being to the girls? They deserve better. They would be better off without me. Gary would be better off without me. Who really cares about me anyway?*

I'd become a raging bitch to my family and my friends, and I thought they wouldn't miss me. I didn't have any parents to reach out to, and I didn't want people to see me like that.

So, fuck it! I decided, *I'm just going to keep on drinking to numb all these feelings.* I would have a good Bloody Mary to start my day, vodka to keep me going, and several big glasses of wine to cap my night off. Sure, that would take care of everything. I wouldn't feel any of those feelings anymore.

Eventually, I realized that I was even more exhausted than ever. I couldn't fall asleep, my nerves were buzzing, and the alcohol wasn't working any more. I decided I needed something else and I knew I had some pain killers in the house somewhere. Rock bottom was the thought running through my head:

*I really don't want to wake up tomorrow.*

*Maybe I could run into a tree or fly off a cliff.*

I was thinking of anything to help stop the pain inside of me, the overwhelming sadness that has taken over my life. I quit. I was not as tough as everyone thought I was. I was not a badass. I was no longer street wise and alley raised. I was kidding myself and everyone around me. I was a loser, a depressed, lonely, stupid, mean bitch, and I was done.

I found those pills. I put them in my hand and just looked at them, and thought, *This is it.* But then something happened, I lost it, I was sobbing uncontrollably like a baby, thinking, *What am I doing?* I cannot do this to my family and my friends. What will people think? I had to do something. I knew I was stronger than that.

I looked at those pills one last time and threw them in the toilet. I was done crying, I was done feeling sorry for myself, I was exhausted trying to keep everyone around me happy. It was MY fucking turn to live life the way I wanted to, or I was going to die. That mini badass was still in there and she was done with the bullshit, done with being a people pleaser. I had to stand up for myself and decide to make different choices.

Choices that made me happy

It was my turn and I was ready.

## TO BE CONTINUED

# EPILOGUE

So you can see, I started out as a mini badass, went through some shit, and became a strong little girl. I wanted to go to college, but got derailed from that, and then I became a people pleasing mother who gave up on herself. Forty-eight years into my life I finally decided to follow my soul's purpose and go for what I truly desired.

Talk about ups and downs, now I had to change the whole way I was living. I had to discover who Kelly really was. I had to get my health in order and then make choices that made me happy. We are strong, spiritual beings, connected to a power that can get us through anything that comes our way. Trust me, I have learned that over and over again. So that is what I'll share in my next book, about how my Inner Badass saved my life. I invite you to follow me through my journey of discovery, fear, doubt and countless *What The Fuck?* moments. Trust me, it'll be worth it.